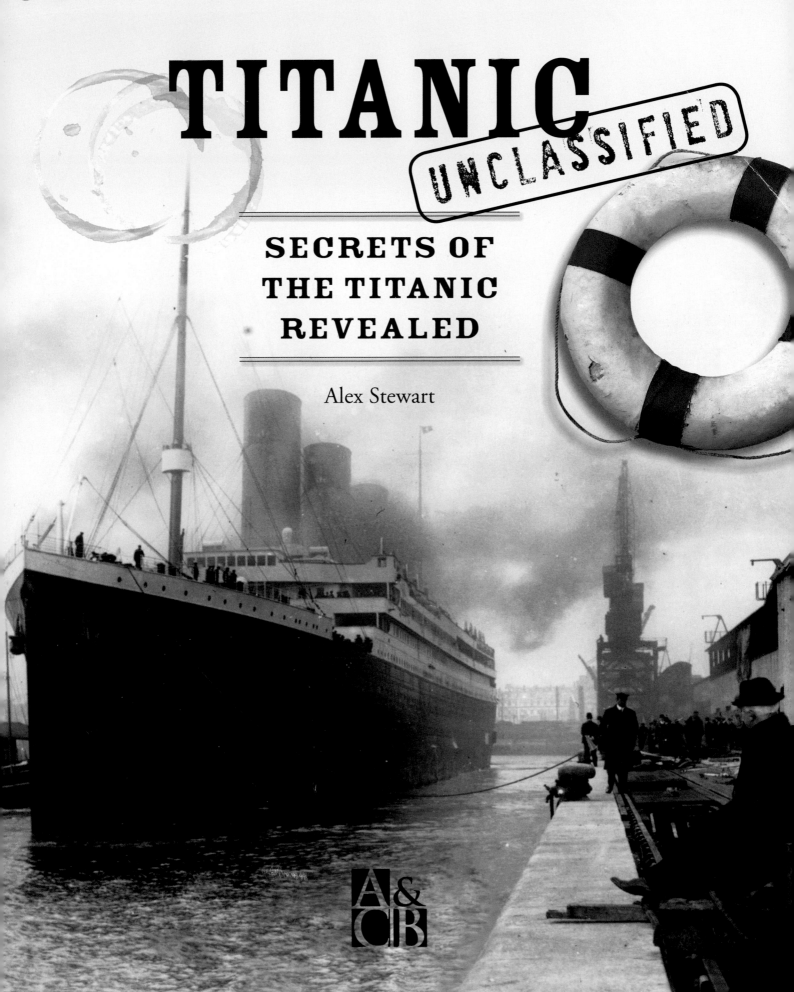

The National Archives

TITANIC
UNCLASSIFIED

SECRETS OF THE TITANIC REVEALED

Alex Stewart

The National Archives

A&CB

Published 2012 by A & C Black, an imprint of
Bloomsbury Publishing Plc, 50 Bedford Square
London, W1CB 3DP

www.acblack.com

Produced for A & C Black by:

White-Thomson Publishing Ltd.
0843 208 7460
www.wtpub.co.uk

ISBN: 978-1-4081-6052-7

A CIP catalogue for this book is available from the British Library.

To see our full range of books
visit www.acblack.com

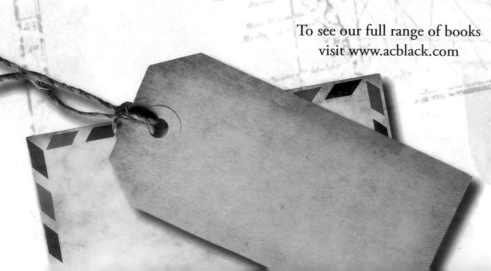

CONTENTS

TRAGEDY

One morning, 100 years ago, news began to come in around the world of a truly horrible disaster. Sailing from Europe to North America, the RMS *Titanic* – one of the largest ships in the world – had collided with an iceberg and sunk on its maiden voyage. More than 1,500 passengers and crew died in the freezing ocean. The terrible tragedy shocked the whole world.

So many questions

At the time, many people simply did not believe that the *Titanic* could have sunk. The brand new ship had been built to the highest safety standards of that time. The crew were skilled, the sea was flat calm. In such conditions, how on earth could such a marvel of modern technology have failed?

Was there a fault in the ship's design? Was it on the wrong course? Could the disaster have been avoided? After the shock and sorrow came anger. Why, when the ship had taken more than two hours to sink, had so few passengers been saved? There was fury, too, at the type of passenger that survived.

▼ In her full working glory, the *Titanic* was an impressive sight.

WHITE STAR LINE.

▲ The bow of the great *Titanic* lies rusting on the ocean floor, seen only by passing fish and occasional divers.

Relatives and friends of the deceased demanded to know why first-class passengers had a better chance of survival than those travelling in second and third class. Others asked why relatively more American than British passengers had been rescued.

Searching for answers

One hundred years have passed since that fateful night when the mighty *Titanic* sank beneath the icy Atlantic Ocean. Inquiries have been held, theories and facts examined, questions asked, and some answers given. The wreck itself has been located on the ocean floor. The fascinating – and sometimes shocking – results of these investigations are set out before you in the pages that follow.

▲ The front page of the *New York Herald* on 15 April 1912. The figures were not accurate, but the message was.

ACROSS THE OCEAN

The *Titanic*'s sinking is one of the key events in the history of transatlantic travel. The Vikings made the first recorded Atlantic crossing more than 1,000 years ago, sailing from Europe to America via Iceland and Greenland. In 1492, Christopher Columbus was captain of the first non-stop crossing, a dangerous voyage of several weeks in a sailing ship. More than 300 years later, in 1838, a new era of transatlantic travel began – the steamship *Sirius* made the journey in just 18 days. Businesspeople, holidaymakers, and emigrating families could all now cross the Atlantic much more quickly and easily.

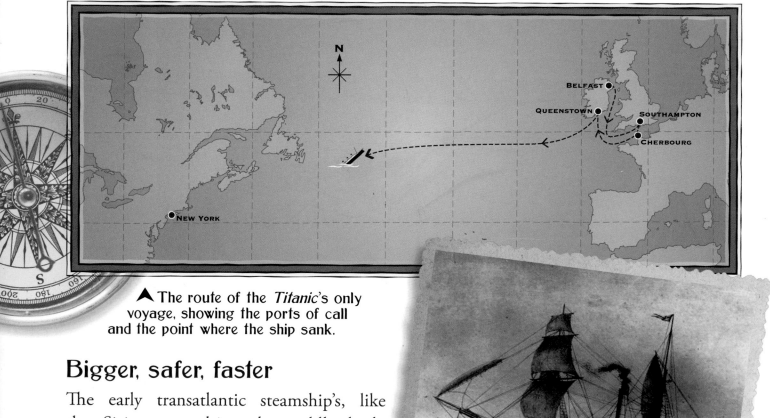

▲ The route of the *Titanic*'s only voyage, showing the ports of call and the point where the ship sank.

Bigger, safer, faster

The early transatlantic steamship's, like the *Sirius*, were driven by paddlewheels on either side of the wooden hull. The vessels were small and carried only a few hundred passengers. Three important developments meant ocean-going vessels were bigger, safer, and faster. Paddlewheels were replaced by more powerful screws (propellers), riveted steel plates – rather than wooden planks – were used to construct hulls, and steam turbines took over from piston-driven steam engines.

▲ The shape of things to come – the 715-tonne SS *Sirius*, which took just 18 days to cross the Atlantic in 1838.

The age of the ocean liner

By the end of the 19th century, Atlantic crossings were more important than ever. The USA was now one of the wealthiest countries in the world, attracting hundreds of thousands of European immigrants each year. To meet the demand, ocean 'liners' – so called because the shipping companies that owned the vessels were known as 'lines' – became larger than ever.

Height of luxury

Wealthy passengers were willing to pay handsomely to travel in great luxury aboard these huge new ships. The 32,000-tonne RMS *Lusitania*, launched by the Cunard Line in 1906, offered 'regal suites' that included two bedrooms, a dining room, a parlour, and a bathroom. Not to be outdone, the White Star Line launched the RMS *Olympic*, the first of their deluxe 46,000-tonne super-liners, in 1911. It was followed the next year by an even heavier sister ship, the RMS *Titanic*.

▲ This White Star Line poster was designed to make its new super-liners seem as big and impressive as possible.

▼ For a short time, the RMS *Olympic* was the largest liner in the world.

Designing the *Titanic*

The White Star Line designed and built three *Olympic*-class liners: the *Olympic*, the *Titanic* and the *Britannic*. They were not as fast as their Cunard rivals, the *Lusitania* and the *Mauretania*, but they were bigger and more luxurious. The first-class facilities were as good as a five-star hotel, and second-class and third-class passengers were remarkably well provided for. The liners also had to look good on the outside – a factor that would play an important part in the *Titanic* tragedy.

Top designers

The plans for the *Titanic* were drawn up by two of the finest ship designers of the time, Lord Pirrie and Thomas Andrews. Pirrie, an extremely successful businessman and politician, was a director of the White Star Line and ran the renowned Harland and Wolff shipyard in Belfast.

Andrews had spent most of his working life designing ships. He came along on the *Titanic*'s maiden voyage, and went down with the ship. A third designer, Alexander Carlisle, was responsible for the *Titanic*'s decoration and equipment.

◀ The *Titanic*'s deck plans were changed and added to by different people.

The design blueprints for the ship's upper deck.

Thomas Andrews (1873–1912), one of the *Titanic*'s designers, was probably the first man to realise the ship would sink, once the extent of the iceberg damage became clear.

Built by the best

The *Titanic* was built in Northern Ireland, in the yard of Harland and Wolff, which at the time was the biggest shipbuilding company in the world. As Lord Pirrie was chairman of Harland and Wolff, his shipyard was the obvious place for the construction of the *Titanic*.

Looking good

Appearance mattered in a ship that prized itself on being the height of luxury. Because four funnels were said to be more impressive than three, the *Titanic* was fitted with a fourth funnel used only for ventilation.

More importantly, the number of lifeboats on the vessel was reduced from 64 to just 20, which was still more than the number required by law for a ship of the *Titanic*'s size. This was done to keep the decks uncluttered and to make the ship look more streamlined. We do not know for certain who made this fateful decision.

Workmen leaving the Harland and Wolff shipyard in Belfast, with the *Titanic* under construction in the background.

THE BIGGEST AND BEST

Three thousand workers laboured for three years (1909–11) to construct the *Titanic*, the world's biggest liner at the time. It cost about £1.5 million (around $7.5 million at the 1912 rate of exchange) to build. In today's money, this would be around £258 million ($400 million). The money came from the company managed by the millionaire US banker J.P. Morgan. No short cuts were taken – the owners and designers wanted their vessel to be the finest ever seen.

How fast did it go?

Top speed:
23 knots
(43 kmh or
26 mph)

What was it made of?

The hull was made of the best steel available – the workers called it 'battleship quality'. However, the steel at the time contained more sulphur than today, which may have made it brittle in icy conditions. The individual steel plates that made up the hull were joined together with rivets – almost 3 million of them – driven in by hydraulic hammers.

How was it powered?

The *Titanic* had three main engines, and two smaller ones to power the steering. Two of the large engines were conventional four-cylinder steam engines. Each powered a three-blade screw (propeller) made of bronze. The third

How big was the *Titanic*?

Height (keel to funnel top): 53.3 m (175 ft)
Weight: 47,071 tonnes

engine was a more modern steam turbine. This drove a central third propeller placed between the other two. The steam to drive the engines was generated in 29 huge boilers heated by 159 furnaces. These coal-burning furnaces were loaded by hand with 840 tonnes of coal per day – hot and dangerous work.

How was it steered?

The ship's massive rudder, measuring 37 sq m (401 sq ft), was moved by two steering engines. One was in regular use, and the second was in reserve in case the other broke down. In an emergency, the rudder could be hand-operated using ropes and winches.

How many people could it carry?

The ship could carry 3,547 passengers and crew members

▲ This picture of the *Titanic*, shortly before its launch, shows the enormous wooden props that kept the ship's hull upright while it was being built.

▼ The structure of the *Titanic* was designed to be both technically superior and visually stunning.

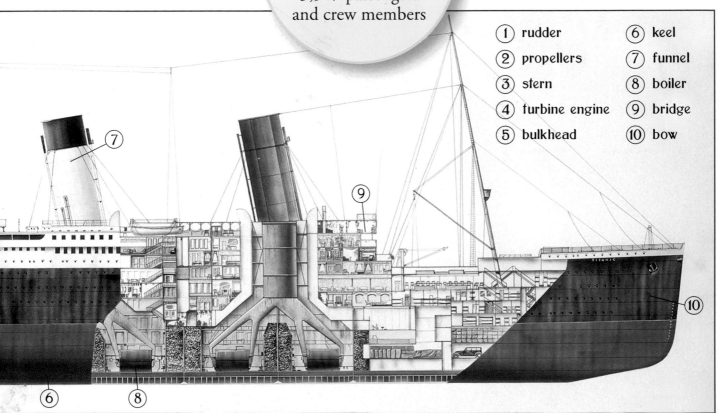

① rudder	⑥ keel
② propellers	⑦ funnel
③ stern	⑧ boiler
④ turbine engine	⑨ bridge
⑤ bulkhead	⑩ bow

TRAVELLING IN STYLE

Titanic's first-class passengers were not the only ones to enjoy top-quality accommodation. The White Star Line wanted all aboard – in first, second, and third class – to have a better transatlantic experience than that offered by the company's rivals. First-class travellers paid up to £870 ($4,350) for a one-way ticket that allowed them to travel in great luxury. This would be around £53,500 ($83,200) in today's money. Second-class passengers paying £12 ($60) and those in third class paying as little as £3 ($15) also had better facilities than on any other liner.

A floating palace

The list of facilities available to first-class passengers is remarkable even by today's standards. Some of the 416 cabins (or 'state rooms') had open coal-burning fires. The *Titanic* was the first ship to boast a heated swimming pool. The gym was fitted with a rowing machine, an exercise bike, and even an electric horse! Elsewhere there was a steam room, squash court, library, French café, dining rooms, smoking rooms, and a darkroom where amateur photographers could develop their pictures.

▼ The *Titanic*'s first-class rooms were stocked with luxury toileteries, as shown in this advert.

▲ Passengers in first class kept fit in the gym.

◄ The *Titanic*'s first-class staterooms were fit for royalty.

▲ Oo la-la! The ship's French-style *Café Parisien* was an elegant spot to relax.

Second class

There were two types of second-class stateroom, and 162 of these rooms in total. The majority had bunk beds, but there were some – for those travelling on their own – that had a single bed and a sofa-style seat. Although second-class passengers had to share a toilet, their rooms had mirrors and basins for washing. They also had their own dining rooms and relaxation areas, separated from both first- and third-class passengers.

> " *The White Star Line has done much to increase the attractions of second-class accommodation during recent years, having made a special feature of this in a number of their vessels; and in the* Olympic *and* Titanic *it will be found that this class of passenger has been generously provided for.*
>
> White Star Line publicity "

Third class

Most third-class passengers paid between £3 ($15) and £8 ($40) for a one-way adult ticket. This was quite a large expense, as in 1912 a good working-class wage was £1.50 ($7.50) per week. Unlike the large dormitories in most emigrant ships, single men and women were housed in one of the 262 four-person cabins equipped with bunk beds and basins. Families occupied the larger but equally comfortable eight-bed rooms in the centre of the ship. For most third-class passengers, life on the *Titanic* was much more comfortable than it had been back home, and than it would be on arrival in the USA. For instance, the *Titanic* was equipped throughout with electric lights, which many in third class would not have had in their own homes.

'DESIGNED TO BE UNSINKABLE'

Neither the *Titanic*'s captain, nor its designers, nor its owners, ever boasted that their ship was 'unsinkable'. They were proud men, but they were not foolish. As the vessel featured almost every safety device available at the time, the White Star Line claimed the *Titanic* was 'designed to be unsinkable'. The company knew it would take either an act of war or an extraordinary combination of circumstances and bad luck to cause their ship to sink.

Emergency measures

An iron ship sinks quickly when its hull is damaged and water floods in. To minimise this risk, the *Titanic*'s hull was divided into 16 compartments. These were separated by watertight walls, known as bulkheads, which rose up from the keel to the lowest deck (see diagram on pp10–11).

▼ Advertisements for the *Titanic* emphasised the ship's great size and power, adding to its reputation for being 'unsinkable'.

In an emergency, the electric doors in these bulkheads could be closed in a matter of seconds, effectively turning the vessel into 16 mini-ships. The *Titanic* could stay afloat even if 4 of the 16 compartments were flooded. The ship was fitted with eight pumps, which together could remove 1,730 tonnes of water from the vessel every hour.

The crew also had two of the most powerful radios available at the time. In an emergency, these could transmit messages many hundreds of miles, calling for help from nearby ships.

▼ The most up-to-date radio equipment from 1912, as used aboard the *Titanic*.

WHITE STAR LINE

T.S.S. TITANIC.

Lifeboats and lifejackets

Finally, if the worst came to the worst, and passengers and crew had to abandon ship, the *Titanic* carried a lifejacket for everyone on board. There were also 49 lifebuoys (floating rings that people can hold on to in the water) and 20 lifeboats. There were fewer lifeboats than originally intended, only enough to take 1,178 persons in total – approximately a third of the ship's full capacity. However, given all the ship's other safety features, no one imagined the lifeboats would ever be needed.

▶ A lifejacket from the *Titanic*. It kept the user afloat – but not warm.

▲ The top deck of the ship was partly lined with lifeboats.

LAUNCH AND TRIALS

The *Titanic* was launched in Belfast, Northern Ireland, on 31 May 1911. It was a magnificent occasion. Special viewing platforms were erected so crowds could watch the great ship slide slowly down the slipway into the water. American and British flags fluttered overhead, while signal flags spelt out the message 'Good Luck'. After the launch, parties, lunches, and dinners were held all over Belfast to celebrate the historic event.

Early tragedy

One Belfast family was not celebrating that afternoon. Shipyard worker James Dobbins had the job of knocking away the wooden supports around the *Titanic*'s hull as it was launched. The ship was then one of the largest moveable objects ever made, and its supporting timbers were as big as trees. As one fell, it injured James very badly, and he died in hospital shortly afterwards.

▶The *Titanic* begins its long-awaited sea trials.

Fitting out

The ship floating high in the Laffan River was little more than a partitioned hull containing engines, boilers, and furnaces. The long process of 'fitting out' now began. This meant building the rooms inside the ship, and making them ready for people to stay in. The process took a whole year. First, the superstructure, cabins, public rooms, and staircases were constructed. Then came plumbers and electricians to install miles of pipework and cabling, followed by carpenters, carpet fitters, and painters. Finally, the moveable objects were loaded on. These ranged from thousands of tonnes of coal to the bed linen, plates, pots, and pans.

Sea trials

On Tuesday 2 April 1912, just eight days before the ship began its maiden voyage out of Southampton, tugboats guided the *Titanic* into open water, steam was fed to the mighty engines, and for the first time the great ship sailed under its own power. On board were 199 crew members, some dignitaries and officials, and a Board of Trade surveyor. It was the latter's job to see that everything worked, so he could give the *Titanic* a certificate of seaworthiness. By 8 p.m. that evening, having seen the ship stop, start, turn sharply to port and starboard, drop anchor, and steam at full speed, the surveyor signed the certificate. The *Titanic* was now officially seaworthy.

Launch
OF
White Star Royal Mail Triple-Screw Steamer
"TITANIC"
At BELFAST,
Wednesday, 31st May, 1911, at 12-15 p.m.

Admit Bearer.

▲ Ticket holders only – the launch of the *Titanic* caused great excitement.

SETTING SAIL

The *Titanic* was designed as a multi-purpose ship. The vessel was a floating luxury hotel for the super-rich, and a comfortable means of ocean transport for the middle classes. The *Titanic* also carried many people who were going to live in the USA. It was a mail ship, too, carrying letters, parcels, and other cargo from port to port.

Out of Southampton

Having crossed from Belfast to the English port of Southampton, the *Titanic* waited there for a week while supplies, crew, and passengers came aboard. Around noon on Wednesday 10 April, the vessel cast off from the quay – and came close to disaster even before reaching the open sea. The huge wave made by the *Titanic* caused the liner *New York* to break the ropes that held it and to swing out towards the oncoming *Titanic*. The two ships came within almost a metre of colliding.

▼ All aboard! The *Titanic* waits at Southampton docks to collect passengers for its maiden voyage.

"OLYMPIC" (Triple-Screw), 45,324 Tons.
AND
"TITANIC" (Triple-Screw), 46,328 Tons.
THE LARGEST STEAMERS IN THE WORLD.

SOUTHAMPTON—CHERBOURG—QUEENSTOWN—NEW YORK SERVICE
Calling at QUEENSTOWN (Westbound) and PLYMOUTH (Eastbound).

FROM SOUTHAMPTON.			FROM CHERBOURG.	STEAMER.	FROM NEW YORK. CALLING AT PLYMOUTH AND CHERBOURG.		
Date.	Day.	Sailing hour.	Sailing about 4·30 p.m.		Date.	Day.	Sailing Hour.
1912 Apl. 3	Wed.	Noon	Apl. 3	OLYMPIC	1912 Apl. 13	Sat.	
„ 10	Wed.	Noon	„ 10	TITANIC	„ 20	Sat.	3·0 pm
„ 24	Wed.	Noon	„ 24	OLYMPIC	May 4	Sat.	Noon
May 1	Wed.	Noon	May 1	TITANIC	„ 11	Sat.	Noon
„ 8	Wed.	Noon	„ 8	OCEANIC	„ 18	Sat.	2·0 pm
„ 15	Wed.	Noon	„ 15	OLYMPIC	„ 25	Sat.	Noon
„ 22	Wed.	Noon	„ 22	TITANIC	June 1	Sat.	1·0 pm
„ 29	Wed.	Noon	„ 29	OCEANIC	„ 8	Sat.	Noon
June 5	Wed.	Noon	June 5	OLYMPIC	„ 15	Sat.	Noon
„ 12	Wed.	11·0 am	„ 12	TITANIC	„ 22	Sat.	10·0 am
„ 19	Wed.	Noon	„ 19	OCEANIC	„ 29	Sat.	Noon
„ 26	Wed.	11·0 am	„ 26	OLYMPIC	July 6	Sat.	Noon
July 3	Wed.	Noon	July 3	TITANIC	„ 13	Sat.	10·0 am
„ 10	Wed.	Noon	„ 10	OCEANIC	„ 20	Sat.	Noon
„ 17	Wed.	2·0 pm	„ 17	OLYMPIC	„ 27	Sat.	Noon
„ 24	Wed.	Noon	„ 24	TITANIC	Aug. 3	Sat.	10·0 am
„ 31	Wed.	Noon	„ 31	OCEANIC	„ 10	Sat.	Noon
Aug. 7	Wed.	Noon	Aug. 7	OLYMPIC	„ 17	Sat.	Noon
„ 14	Wed.	Noon	„ 14	TITANIC	„ 24	Sat.	Noon
„ 21	Wed.	Noon	„ 21	OCEANIC	„ 31	Sat.	3·0 pm
„ 28	Wed.	Noon	„ 28	OLYMPIC	Sept. 7	Sat.	Noon
Sept. 4	Wed.	Noon	Sept. 4	TITANIC	„ 14	Sat.	2·0 pm
„ 11	Wed.	Noon	„ 11	OCEANIC	„ 21	Sat.	Noon
„ 18	Wed.	Noon	„ 18	OLYMPIC	„ 28	Sat.	Noon
„ 25	Wed.	Noon	„ 25	TITANIC	Oct. 5	Sat.	Noon
Oct. 9	Wed.	Noon	Oct. 9	OCEANIC	„ 12	Sat.	2·0 pm
„ 16	Wed.	Noon	„ 16	OLYMPIC	„ 19	Sat.	Noon
„ 23	Wed.	Noon	„ 23	TITANIC	„ 26	Sat.	Noon
„ 30	Wed.	Noon	„ 30	OCEANIC	Nov. 2	Sat.	11·0 am
Nov. 6	Wed.	11·0 am	Nov. 6	OLYMPIC	„ 9	Sat.	Noon
„ 13	Wed.	Noon	„ 13	TITANIC	„ 16	Sat.	10·0 am
„ 20	Wed.	2·30 pm	„ 20	OCEANIC	„ 23	Sat.	Noon
„ 27	Wed.	Noon	„ 27	OLYMPIC	„ 30	Sat.	Noon
Dec. 4	Wed.	Noon	Dec. 4	TITANIC	Dec. 7	Sat.	9·0 am
„ 11	Wed.	Noon	„ 11	OCEANIC	„ 14	Sat.	Noon
„ 18	Wed.	1·0 pm	„ 18	OLYMPIC	„ 21	Sat.	3·0 pm
Dec. 25	Wed.	Noon	„ 25	TITANIC	1913 Jan. 4	Sat.	Noon
				OCEANIC			

FIRST CLASS PASSENGER LIST
PER
ROYAL AND U.S. MAIL
S.S. "Titanic,"
FROM SOUTHAMPTON AND CHERBOURG
TO NEW YORK
(Via QUEENSTOWN).

Wednesday, 10th April, 1912.

Captain, E. J. Smith, R.D. (Comm...
Surgeon, W. F. N. O'Loughlin.
Asst. Surgeon, J. E. Simpson.
Chief Stewar... Latimer.

Purser... H. W. McElroy
R. L. Barker.

S Allen, Miss Elizabeth W...
Allison, Mr. H. J.
Allison, Mrs. H. J. and Maid
S Allison, Miss
SS Allison, Master and Nurse
S Anderson, Mr. Harry
S Andrews, Miss Cornelia I.

Andrews, Mr. Thomas
S Appleton, Mrs. E. D.
Artagaveytia, Mr. Ramon
Astor, Colonel J. J. and Manservant
S Astor, Mrs. J. J. and Maid
Aubert, Mrs. N. and Maid

Cherbourg

The first leg of the voyage was 113 km (70 miles) to the French port of Cherbourg. As the *Titanic* was too large for the dock, passengers, mail, and goods had to be carried to and from the shore in small White Star ships known as 'tenders'. That evening, the *Titanic* set sail for the Irish port of Queenstown.

Queenstown – and beyond

At 11.30 a.m. on 11 April, the *Titanic* anchored two miles off Queenstown while a further 120 passengers came aboard in tenders. Seven passengers also disembarked, along with crew member John Coffey, who sneaked ashore to his home port by hiding among the mail bags that were being unloaded. Around lunchtime, the massive anchors were raised for the last time, and the *Titanic* swung out into the Atlantic Ocean, heading for New York.

Passenger numbers

Those getting on and off the ship in different ports were not registered accurately, so we cannot be entirely sure how many people were aboard the *Titanic* when the vessel set out on its final voyage. These figures are the most accurate available to us now:

1st class: 325
2nd class: 285
3rd class: 706
Passenger total: 1,316
Crew: 885

Overall total: 2,211. This was 1,336 fewer than the ship might have been carrying if full to capacity (3,547).

RICH AND FAMOUS

The 325 passengers travelling in the *Titanic*'s first class included some of the richest and most famous people in the world. The majority of the best-known were American. Few of them travelled alone. Most were accompanied not just by their partners and children, but also by their companions, maids, valets, nurses, and even their own cooks!

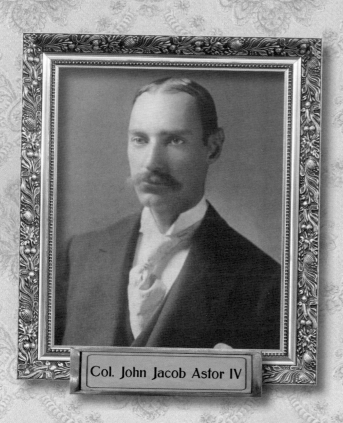

Col. John Jacob Astor IV

Dorothy Gibson

Col. John Jacob Astor IV

The 48-year-old American inventor, writer, and businessman, John Jacob Astor (1864–1912), was one of the world's wealthiest men. His $150 million fortune would be many billions in today's money. He was on board the *Titanic* with his second wife, the 19-year-old Madeleine Talmage Force (1893–1940), who was pregnant. He died in the shipwreck, while his wife survived.

Dorothy Gibson

American actress Dorothy Gibson (1889–1946) was returning to the USA after a holiday in Italy. She began her career as a singer and dancer before shooting to fame in 1911 as one of the first-ever film stars. Rescued by lifeboat 7, she starred in a movie released only a month after the disaster, *Saved from the* Titanic.

Isidor Straus

W. T. Stead

Margaret Brown

Isidor Straus

German-born Isidor Straus (1845–1912) was co-owner of the world's largest store, Macy's. His wife Ida (1849–1912) refused to get into a lifeboat because she didn't want to be parted from him. They both perished.

W. T. Stead

Radical journalist and campaigner for social reform W. T. Stead (1849–1912) was the most famous British passenger. He was travelling to attend a peace conference in America, but never reached his destination.

Margaret Brown

'The Unsinkable Molly Brown' (1867–1932), as she was known after the *Titanic* disaster, was a very wealthy leader of smart American society. She campaigned for women's rights, and for children to be tried in special courts. After helping evacuate passengers during the disaster, she was carried to safety in lifeboat 6.

EMIGRANTS

It is estimated that around 80 per cent of the second- and third-class passengers (about 790 people, 60 per cent of all passengers) were emigrating to the USA. These emigrants came from all over Europe and the Middle East, and even as far as Hong Kong.

Joseph (1886–1912) and Juliette Laroche (1889–1980) were returning to Haiti with their daughters Simonne (1909–73) and Louise (1910–98). The only black people on board, they had left France to avoid racial discrimination. Joseph Laroche did not survive the *Titanic*'s sinking.

Lee Ling (1884–1912), a 28-year-old seaman from Hong Kong, paid an extraordinary £56 for a third-class ticket. Sadly, it did not get him to New York.

Nassef Cassem Albimona (1885–1962) was a salesman from Lebanon, travelling in third class. He had emigrated to the USA in 1903, and was returning there after visiting his wife and children in Lebanon. He was rescued by lifeboat 15.

Hilda Hellström (1889–1962) was 22 years old when she boarded the *Titanic* alone, ready to start a new life in America. She had postponed her move for a long time, staying in her native Sweden to care for her seriously ill mother. After surviving the sinking, Hilda's fear of water was so great that she never returned to Sweden to visit her friends and relatives.

The Goodwin family from England were travelling in third class to Niagara Falls, New York, in search of a better life. Tragically, all eight members of the family went down with the *Titanic*. Their 19-month-old son, Sidney James (not pictured above), was the youngest victim of the disaster.

Michel Navratil (1880–1912), a French tailor, was travelling under the name Louis M. Hoffman. With him were his two sons, Michel (1908–2001) and Edmond (1910–1953), whom he had kidnapped from his wife Marcelle and was taking to America. He died but his sons, who became known as the '*Titanic* Orphans', survived.

THE LAP OF LUXURY

The morning of Friday 12 April dawned bright and clear. The sea was calm, making life for the *Titanic*'s first-class passengers as ideal as they had hoped. With servants, waiters, chambermaids, stewards, and the deck crew catering for their every need, their most pressing worries would be deciding what to wear, avoiding eating and drinking too much, and trying to remember the names of the guests they had met the night before.

A leisurely start

Breakfast in bed, in the elegant first-class dining saloon, or just a cup of fresh coffee in the authentic *Café Parisien*? What a difficult decision! After a turn around the deck in the fresh air, the men would pop into the ornate first-class smoking room for a cigar, while the ladies dropped into the reading room, all awaiting the bugle call announcing that luncheon was being served.

▼ The graceful reading room was the perfect spot for ladies to write their letters.

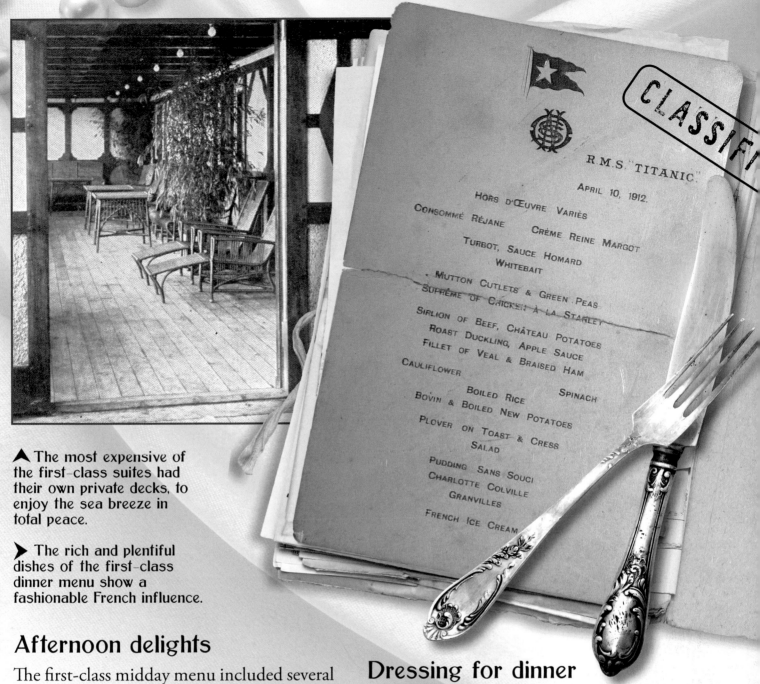

R.M.S. "TITANIC."

APRIL 10, 1912.

HORS D'ŒUVRE VARIÈS
CONSOMMÉ RÉJANE   CRÈME REINE MARGOT
TURBOT, SAUCE HOMARD
WHITEBAIT
MUTTON CUTLETS & GREEN PEAS
SUPRÊME OF CHICKEN A LA STANLEY
SIRLOIN OF BEEF, CHÂTEAU POTATOES
ROAST DUCKLING, APPLE SAUCE
FILLET OF VEAL & BRAISED HAM
CAULIFLOWER   SPINACH
BOILED RICE
BOVIN & BOILED NEW POTATOES
PLOVER ON TOAST & CRESS
SALAD
PUDDING SANS SOUCI
CHARLOTTE COLVILLE
GRANVILLES
FRENCH ICE CREAM

▲ The most expensive of the first-class suites had their own private decks, to enjoy the sea breeze in total peace.

▶ The rich and plentiful dishes of the first-class dinner menu show a fashionable French influence.

Afternoon delights

The first-class midday menu included several kinds of soup, a vast array of vegetables, numerous varieties of meat, and eight types of cheese. Following a short after-lunch nap, first-class passengers would perhaps take another breath of fresh air, play a game of squash, go for a swim, send a wireless message, or even check with the purser that their cargo remained secure. The ship's hold contained such precious items as four cases of opium and a rare jewelled book (the *Rubáiyát* of Omar Khayám) bought just before the voyage for £405.

Dressing for dinner

The evening centred around dinner, a stupendous meal of 11 courses washed down with the very finest wines. In preparation, the ladies dressed in glorious gowns and put on their sparkling jewels, while the men slipped into dinner jackets, waistcoats, and double-ended bow ties (hand-knotted, of course). Before the meal, they would take drinks in the French-style first-class reception room. After the meal came brandy or port, more cigars, and some leisurely conversation.

COMFORT FOR ALL

The *Titanic* was built to make money. To do this, the White Star Line needed it to sail with all cabins occupied – with 2,762 passengers on board, not the 1,316 who took the maiden voyage. The best way to fill the ship was to make sure it was recommended by all who came on board. So, for example, with this in mind a third-class ticket included meals, whereas on other ships passengers paying the lowest fares had to bring their own food.

Second class

For second-class passengers, life on board was not so different from that of those travelling in first class. The state rooms were comfortable, the public rooms lavish, and the meals delicious. When not eating, drinking, or sleeping, passengers had their own promenade deck for exercise, their own library, and smoking room. The White Star Line even provided pushchairs in which young children and babies could be wheeled around the deck.

▼ The White Star Line was keen to show that the *Titanic*'s second-class accommodation was exceptionally comfortable.

Third class

Third-class passengers had centrally-heated cabins, a 'general' room, dining room, smoking room, and open promenade space at the stern of the vessel. All were well equipped. The dining room, for instance, was furnished with individual chairs rather than benches.

What the third-class passenger might have appreciated most was the food – wholesome, and plenty of it. Some of the items, such as fresh oranges and apricots, would have been luxuries that many passengers had never tasted before.

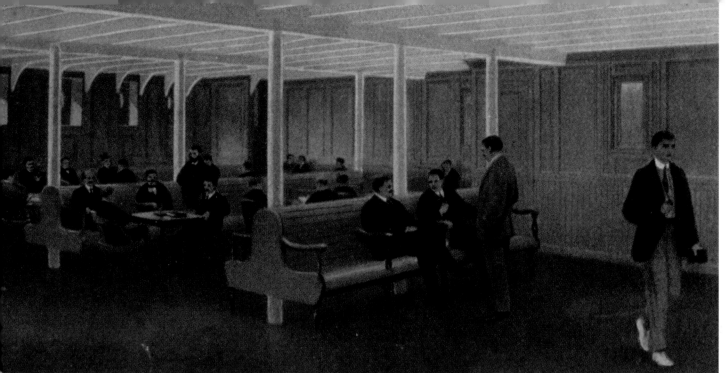

▲ The third-class smoking room, as drawn by a White Star Line artist. Since women were not expected to smoke in public, this was a 'men only' area.

Strict separation

Passengers of different classes were not meant to mingle with each other. To prevent third-class passengers wandering into areas reserved for other classes, certain stairways and doorways were closed by sliding metal grilles. These could easily be opened in an emergency – as long as there was someone on hand with the correct key. Third-class accommodation for single men and women was also at opposite ends of the ship, as it was considered improper for unmarried men and women to sleep near each other.

▶ Four good meals a day were included in the ticket price for third-class passengers.

WHITE STAR LINE.

R.M.S. "TITANIC."

APRIL 14, 1912.

THIRD CLASS.
BREAKFAST.
Oatmeal Porridge & Milk
Smoked Herrings, Jacket Potatoes
Ham & Eggs
Fresh Bread & Butter
Marmalade   Swedish Bread
Tea   Coffee

DINNER.
Rice Soup
Fresh Bread   Cabin Biscuits
Roast Beef, Brown Gravy
Sweet Corn   Boiled Potatoes
Plum Pudding, Sweet Sauce
Fruit

TEA.
Cold Meat
Cheese   Pickles
Fresh Bread & Butter
Stewed Figs & Rice
Tea

SUPPER
Gruel   Cabin Biscuits   Cheese

Any complaint respecting the Food supplied, want of attention or incivility, should be at once reported to the Purser or Chief Steward. For purposes of identification, each Steward wears a numbered badge on the arm.

CREW

The great majority of the *Titanic*'s crew were from Britain or Ireland, although several were American, Canadian, or Western European. A small number of crew members came from countries as far off as Australia, India, Cape Verde, Mexico, and South Africa. The oldest crew member is believed to have been the 62-year-old surgeon, William O'Loughlin, who went down with the ship. The youngest was a 14-year-old bell boy named W. Albert Watson, who survived the sinking.

Captain Edward Smith

Smith (1850–1912) went to sea at the age of 13, and worked his way up to become captain of the world's most famous ship. He was a popular figure. However, when he realised the *Titanic* would sink, some survivors claim he appeared shocked and unable to take full command of the situation. His body was never recovered.

Wallace Hartley

Bandleader Hartley (1878–1912) kept his small orchestra playing even as the water swirled about their feet. None of the musicians survived, and Hartley left a heartbroken fiancée in Wetherby, Yorkshire.

Charles John Joughin

Joughin (above, 1879–1956) was the *Titanic*'s chief baker. He transferred onto the ship from the *Olympic*, and received a monthly wage of £12 (£880 in today's money). After the sinking, Joughin swam up to Lifeboat B and tried to climb in, but there was no room and he was pushed off. He clung to the side of the lifeboat for hours, submerged in the ice-cold water, and miraculously survived. He went on to serve on many other ships throughout his career.

William George White

White (below, born 1888) was a 23-year-old man from Hampshire, England, who worked in the *Titanic*'s engine room. The job title on his identity card is 'Fireman', which means he was one of the crew members responsible for keeping the ship's coal furnaces burning. Records show that White was rescued in Lifeboat 15, but nothing is known of him after this time.

WARNINGS

From time to time, huge pieces of ice – known as icebergs – drift south from the frozen region around the North Pole. They can rise up to 75 m (246 ft) above the ocean and can weigh a remarkable 224,000 tonnes. In other words, a very large iceberg is taller and heavier than any ship ever built. Colliding with a rock-hard iceberg at speed can seriously damage a vessel, sometimes sinking it without a trace.

False accusations

Nowadays, icebergs can be spotted by radar, a device that did not exist in the *Titanic*'s day. To help each other, ships sailing in iceberg zones used radio to pass on information about sightings. Also, when passing through these dangerous waters at night or in fog, ships generally slowed right down or stopped completely. The *Titanic* did neither.

Indeed, some American newspapers falsely accused J. Bruce Ismay, chairman of the White Star Line, of ordering Captain Smith to maintain a high speed (21 knots) in order to show what a swift liner the *Titanic* was.

▼ Danger – ice! A photograph of the precise area where the *Titanic* sank, taken ten days before the disaster.

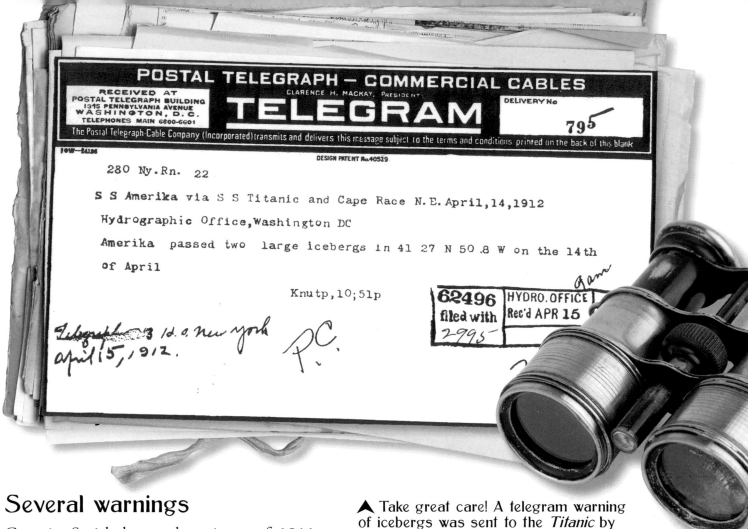

The telegram shown reads:

POSTAL TELEGRAPH — COMMERCIAL CABLES

CLARENCE H. MACKAY, PRESIDENT

TELEGRAM

RECEIVED AT POSTAL TELEGRAPH BUILDING 1315 PENNSYLVANIA AVENUE WASHINGTON, D.C. TELEPHONES MAIN 6600-6601

DELIVERY No 795

The Postal Telegraph-Cable Company (Incorporated) transmits and delivers this message subject to the terms and conditions printed on the back of this blank

DESIGN PATENT Ro.40529

280 Ny.Rn. 22

S S Amerika via S S Titanic and Cape Race N.E. April,14,1912

Hydrographic Office,Washington DC

Amerika passed two large icebergs in 41 27 N 50 .8 W on the 14th of April

Knutp,10;51p

62496 filed with 2-995

HYDRO.OFFICE Rec'd APR 15

Several warnings

Captain Smith knew the winter of 1911–12 had been unusually mild and, as a consequence, ice was drifting further south than normal. He was also told of iceberg sightings by other ships taking roughly the same course as the *Titanic*. Six warnings were received on 11 April, five on 12 April, three on 13 April, and a further seven on Sunday 14 April. Acting on this information, Captain Smith altered the course of his ship a few degrees to the south.

On the evening of Sunday 14 April, the *Mesaba* radioed with a serious iceberg warning. The men operating the *Titanic*'s powerful new radio, Jack Phillips and Harold Bride, were busy sending out passengers' messages to Cape Race, Newfoundland. Disastrously, Phillips did not pass on the most recent iceberg warning to the bridge.

▲ Take great care! A telegram warning of icebergs was sent to the *Titanic* by SS *Amerika* on the day of the disaster.

"

Radio operator Harold Bride admitted not recording an ice warning from the steamship *Californian* sent on the afternoon of Sunday 14 April.

Solicitor General: The message from the Californian … refers to the three icebergs, and gave the latitude and longitude?

Bride: Yes …

SG: Did you write it down?

B: No, the first time I did not take it down.

SG: It came to your ears?

B: It came to my ears, yes … I took no notice of it.

SG Because you were busy you took no notice of it?

B: Yes.

"

COLLISION

A good number of stories have emerged from the night the *Titanic* went down – some of courage, a few of cowardice, and many of good people doing their duty in tragic circumstances. Most questions have been answered, although others will forever remain a mystery. There are certain facts we know for sure. The first and undoubtedly most important is that precisely 37 seconds after 11.40 p.m. on Sunday 14 April, RMS *Titanic* collided with a huge iceberg.

In the crow's nest

Frederick Fleet and Reginald Lee took up their lookout positions in the crow's nest of the *Titanic* at 10 p.m. Neither man had been issued with binoculars. As the night drew on, they noticed a haze rising over the sea. Coupled with the lack of moonlight that night, this visibility issue made their job difficult. Nevertheless, warned that there were icebergs in the area, they kept their eyes peeled.

Iceberg!

Fleet saw it first, a vast blue-black shape rising out of the water about 450 m (1475 ft) straight in front of them. Steaming along at 21–22 knots, the *Titanic* had about 30 seconds to alter course and avoid hitting the iceberg head on.

Fleet gave the alarm, ringing the ship's bell three times, and called the bridge – "Iceberg, right ahead!" First Officer Will Murdoch gave the order, "Hard-a-starboard!", so that the liner swerved to port (left). However, there was no way the ship could steer completely clear of the iceberg.

The fatal moment

The starboard (right) bow of the *Titanic* crunched along the iceberg for about ten seconds. The collision was felt by the crew in the forward part of the ship, but many passengers noticed nothing at all. It was close to midnight and the majority of them were fast asleep.

▼ The US Coastguard issued the first official report of the collision.

COLLISION WITH ICEBERG – Apr 14 – Lat 41° 46', lon 50° 14', the British steamer TITANIC collided with an iceberg seriously damaging her bow; extent not definitely known.

Apr 14 – The German steamer AMERIKA reported by radio telegraph passing two large icebergs in lat 41° 27', lon 50° 08',––TITANIC (Br ss).

Apr 14 – Lat 42° 06', lon 49° 43', encountered extensive field ice and saw seven icebergs of considerable size.––PISA (Ger ss).

J. J. KNAPP

Captain, U. S. Navy,
Hydrographer.

'MATHEMATICAL CERTAINTY'

The slight judder that ran through the ship as it struck the iceberg might not have been noticed by many of the passengers, but to an experienced sailor like Captain Smith it was an ominous sensation. He hurried to the bridge, found out what had happened, made sure the engines were stopped, and set about assessing the damage.

"

Third Officer Bert Pitman recalls the collision:

Mr. Pitman: *Well, the collision woke me up.*

Senator Smith: W*as there any special impact to awaken you?*

P: *No; there was a sound that I thought seemed like the ship coming to an anchor – the chain running out over the windlass.*

SS: *Did this impact jar the ship?*

P: *No; it gave just a little vibration. I was about half awake and about half asleep. It did not quite awaken me.*

"

▲ Third Officer Bert Pitman (1877–1961) and Second Officer Charles Lightoller (1874–1952) were key witnesses at the inquiries into the *Titanic*'s sinking.

Six gashes

After a quick look at the front of the ship, Fourth Officer Joseph Boxall said things did not seem too serious. But when a carpenter, possibly 26-year-old John Hutchinson, and the ship's principal designer, Thomas Andrews, made a closer inspection, the true extent of the damage became horribly clear. The force of the liner crashing against the iceberg opened six gashes in the ship's side along a distance of 90 m (299 ft). There seem to have been two reasons for such serious damage. First, the low temperature made the *Titanic*'s steel likely to break rather than bend. Second, the ship's steel plates were joined to each other and to the main frame by rivets. Under enormous strain, these rivets simply broke or popped out. The resulting holes allowed seawater to pour into 6 of the vessel's 16 compartments.

Slowly filling up

By midnight, Andrews and the carpenter had finished their inspection and reported back to Captain Smith on the bridge. The news was bad. The ship was designed to stay afloat with four compartments flooded, but not six. The pumps, which were steam-powered and only worked for a limited period of time, could not cope. They needed an hour to pump out the quantity of water entering the ship every five minutes. Worse still, as the forward compartments filled, water began to pour over the top of them into the compartments behind. Grim-faced, Andrews announced that it was a 'mathematical certainty' that the *Titanic* would sink. How long had they got? asked the captain. Andrews reckoned about an hour.

▼ With the help of L.P. Skidmore, survivor John B. Thayer drew this diagram of the *Titanic*'s sinking immediately after he was rescued. The sequence of events it shows is controversial, as there was debate over how the ship sank.

▲ Even the mighty *Titanic* couldn't survive a collision with an iceberg the size of a small island.

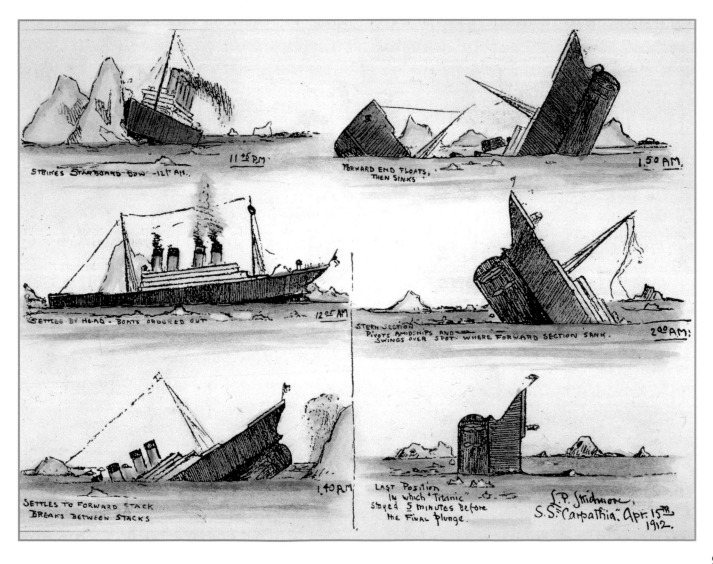

DISTRESS SIGNALS

By midnight, the water had reached the mail room, 7.3 m (24 ft) above the keel. As the forward part of the ship sank lower, the stern rose, eventually exposing the massive propellers. The captain gave orders for the crew to send out distress signals, prepare the lifeboats and assemble the passengers on deck in their lifejackets.

Help!

Acting on the captain's orders, Jack Phillips and Harold Bride began to send out radio distress calls. The messages gave the *Titanic*'s position and asked for assistance as quickly as possible.

The liner's powerful new radio equipment meant that the signals reached at least six ships, and the nearest land base in Cape Race, Canada.

▲ The *Titanic*'s senior radio officer, 25-year-old Jack Phillips (1887–1912), was sending out signals for help almost until the moment the liner sank.

◀ The *Titanic*'s communications room. The equipment, installed by the Marconi Company, was the best available at the time.

Rockets

Slightly more than an hour after striking the iceberg, the *Titanic* tried a second, more desperate, cry for help. Perhaps as many as eight white rockets – a well-known sign of distress – were fired into the air.

Fourth Officer Joseph Boxall saw the lights of another vessel nearby and used a signal lamp to flash a message of distress. There was no reply, although the ship must have seen the *Titanic*'s rockets. It seems fairly certain that the mystery ship was the *Californian* (see pp 38–39).

Response

By this time, however, help was on its way. The *Carpathia* had picked up the *Titanic*'s messages 93 km (58 miles) away and was now rushing flat out to the scene.

Other ships reacted less urgently. Both the *Frankfurt* and the *Birma* insisted on first asking 'What's the matter with you?' Many of those in charge, it seemed, could not believe that the *Titanic* was really going down.

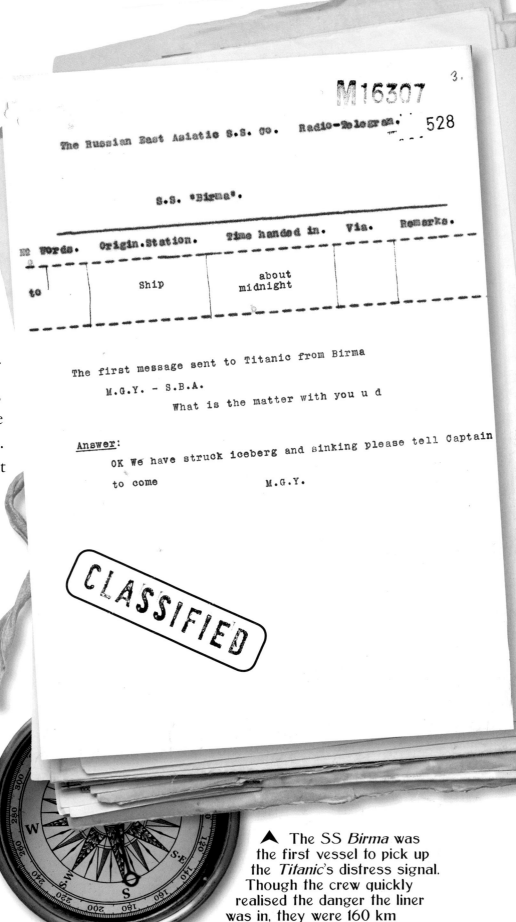

M16307   3.

The Russian East Asiatic S.S. Co.   Radio-Telegram.   528

S.S. "Birma".

No Words.	Origin.Station.	Time handed in.	Via.	Remarks.
to	Ship	about midnight		

The first message sent to Titanic from Birma
    M.G.Y. - S.B.A.
            What is the matter with you u d

Answer:
    OK We have struck iceberg and sinking please tell Captain
to come   M.G.Y.

CLASSIFIED

▲ The SS *Birma* was the first vessel to pick up the *Titanic*'s distress signal. Though the crew quickly realised the danger the liner was in, they were 160 km (100 miles) away and unable to come to the rescue in time.

THE CALIFORNIAN

As the sinking *Titanic* frantically signalled for help, only a few miles off another ship lay idly by, unaware of what was happening. The merchant ship *Californian*, travelling from London to Boston, USA, had run into an area of dangerous ice earlier that evening. The vessel's captain, Stanley Lord, decided it was safer to stop the engines and wait for dawn before proceeding.

Failed contact

As the *Californian* lay there in the calm, freezing water, both Captain Lord and one of his officers saw the lights of a large ship nearby. Lord suggested the ship be contacted by signal lamp. This was done, but no response came.

Lord also asked his only radio operator, Cyril Evans, which ships were nearby. When told 'only the *Titanic*', he asked Evans to inform the vessel of the *Californian*'s situation. Evans tried, but aboard the *Titanic* Jack Phillips was busy sending passengers' messages. Annoyed at Evans's signal interrupting his own, he told the *Californian* to 'Shut up!' Shortly afterwards, Evans turned off his radio and went to bed.

▲ Captain Stanley Lord was criticised by some after the *Titanic* disaster.

White rockets

About an hour after the *Titanic*'s collision, Herbert Stone, the *Californian*'s Second Officer, saw a succession of white rockets in the direction of a ship he too had tried to contact by signal lamp. James Gibson, an apprentice, joined him on the bridge and they discussed what they had seen. Half an hour after seeing the rockets, Stone informed the captain. Lord, who did not seem very concerned, asked a few questions and went back to sleep.

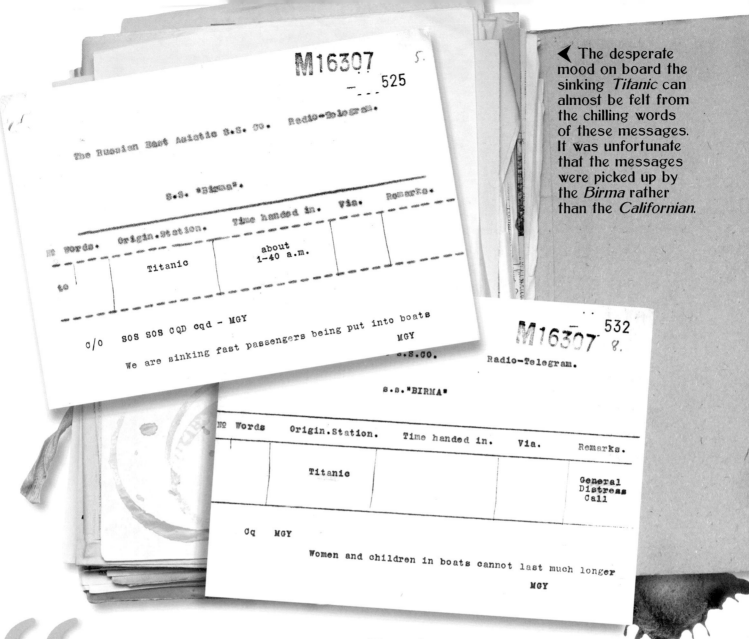

The desperate mood on board the sinking *Titanic* can almost be felt from the chilling words of these messages. It was unfortunate that the messages were picked up by the *Birma* rather than the *Californian*.

James Gibson recalls the conversation he had on the night the *Titanic* sank:

The Second Officer remarked to me, 'Look at her now; she looks very queer out of the water; her lights look queer.'

I looked at her through the glasses after that, and her lights did not seem to be natural ... She seemed as if she had a heavy list to starboard.

Second Officer Stone remarked to me that a ship was not going to fire rockets at sea for nothing.

We were talking about it ... till five minutes past two, when she disappeared.

Evasion

Later that night, the duty watchman on the *Californian* saw the *Carpathia* rushing – too late – to the *Titanic*'s rescue. Woken at 5.30 a.m., Evans switched on his radio and learned of the dreadful events of the night.

For reasons that have never been explained, Captain Lord then steered his ship away from the disaster zone for a while before returning. By the time the *Californian* reached the scene of the tragedy, the *Carpathia* had collected all the survivors, and only debris and empty lifeboats remained.

LIFEBOATS

When a liner sinks very slowly in a flat-calm sea, one would expect the great majority of those on board to be saved. This was not the case with the *Titanic*, and there are two principal reasons why so few survived. First, there were not enough lifeboats for all passengers and crew members on board, and the loading of those available was badly managed. Second, the bitterly cold temperature of the air and sea meant people could not last long in the water.

Unprepared

If all the lifeboats that had left the ship had been filled to capacity, many more people might have been saved. The disorganised loading of the boats was largely due to poor planning.

Sunday's lifeboat drill (a practice for an emergency) had been cancelled – perhaps to allow passengers to go to church. Also, orders to prepare the lifeboats didn't go out until 25 minutes after the collision. At the same time, the crew began waking the passengers and assembling them on the deck.

▶This table explains what happened to each lifeboat.

Lifeboat no.	Capacity	Approx. no. of people aboard (no. of crew)	Time launched (a.m.)
A	47	13 (4)	2.20 (floats off, flooded. Eight die of cold during the night, one moves to boat 14)
B	47	30 (19)	2.20 (floats off upside down with men clinging to it)
C	47	45 (7)	1.40 (Joseph B. Ismay, President of the White Star Line, was on this boat)
D	47	22 (3)	2.05
1	40	12 (7)	1.00 (Five first-class passengers and seven crew members aboard – great scandal)
2	40	18 (5)	1.45
3	65	39 (12)	1.00
4	65	40 (10)	1.55 (Seven swimmers pulled aboard, two die)
5	65	35 (7)	12.55
6	65	25 (5)	12.55
7	65	28 (3)	12.45 (first boat to be lowered)
8	65	28 (4)	1.10
9	65	41 (15)	1.20
10	65	28 (4)	1.20
11	65	50 (26)	1.45
12	65	22 (2)	1.25
13	65	63 (24)	1.30
14	65	43 (10)	1.30 (Returned to scene of sinking and picked up four survivors – one died)
15	65	59 (25)	1.35
16	65	38 (12)	1.35

Another problem was that some people refused to get into the lifeboats. They either did not believe the *Titanic* was sinking, or they were men who felt women and children should be rescued before them.

Captain's failing

At this point, Captain Smith should have given clear and precise orders about filling and launching the boats. He did not. No one was sure where to go and what to do.

Men were turned back from half-full boats as women and children were given priority. The first boat (lifeboat 7) was not lowered into the sea until 12.45 a.m. It contained just 28 people, despite having a maximum capacity of 65.

▶ This picture from the *Illustrated London News* of May 1912 shows men allowing women and children to get into the lifeboats before them.

At the British inquiry, Second Officer Charles Lightoller defended launching half-empty lifeboats:

Q: In your judgment is it possible to fill these lifeboats when they are hanging as full as you might fill them when they are water borne?

A: Most certainly not ... I certainly should not think that the lifeboats would carry it without some structural damage being done - buckling, or something like that.

Q: And had you those considerations in mind in deciding how many people should go in the boat?

A: Yes.

THE *TITANIC*'S LAST MOMENTS

At 1.30 a.m. on Sunday 14 April, almost two hours after striking the iceberg, it is clear that the *Titanic* will not remain afloat much longer. There are signs of panic, and Fifth Officer Harold Lowe fires his pistol into the air to stop passengers jumping into an already-full lifeboat. Still in the radio room, Jack Phillips signals desperately, 'We are sinking fast … Cannot last much longer.'

" 19-year-old Helen Bishop, among the newlyweds given priority, tells of her escape in Lifeboat 7:

We had no idea that it was time to get off, but the officer took my arm and told me to be very quiet and get in immediately. They put the families in the first two boats. My husband was pushed in with me, and we were lowered away with 28 people in the boat. "

Trapped inside

Half an hour later, the forward part of the liner is entirely submerged and the stern is rising out of the sea. Collapsible Lifeboat D gets away, half-full. Below decks, hundreds of passengers and crew trapped by the rising water have already drowned. Some of the third-class passengers are unable to get on deck – although they are not deliberately trapped, no crew member is available to unlock the grilles isolating their part of the ship.

The band plays on

The ship's orchestra is on deck, playing cheerful tunes almost to the end. Finally, their tone becomes sadder. Afterwards, some survivors say the final number was *Nearer my God to Thee*, while others remember *Songe d'Automne* (*Autumn Dream*). As all the band

members died, we will never know for sure. Captain Smith is last seen on the bridge, unwilling to save himself. Thomas Andrews, the ship's designer, sits gazing at a painting in the first-class smoking room. Having been refused permission to join his pregnant wife in a lifeboat, millionaire J.J. Astor stands on deck, patiently waiting for the end.

Finale

At around 2.10 a.m., the propellers rise out of the water. Shortly afterwards, as the sea swirls around the boat deck, the last two collapsible lifeboats (A and B) float clear. One of the massive funnels then breaks off, crushing survivors struggling in the water. The stern rises higher and higher until the great ship cracks in two under the strain, and the forward section disappears into the inky depths. The stern floats normally for a few moments before it too stands vertically and dives down towards the seabed 4 km (2.5 miles) below.

Icy waters

Many passengers fell or jumped from the sinking *Titanic* into the freezing ocean. Most of the lifeboats rowed quickly away from the ship because they feared either being swamped by passengers struggling in the water, or being sucked down underwater as the liner sank. As a result, few survivors were pulled from the water. As it turned out, the ship going down didn't cause enough suction to sink the lifeboats.

Colonel Archibald Gracie recalls swimming for his life:

When I got under water, I struck out with all my strength to the surface … Dying men and women all about me were groaning and crying piteously. By moving from one piece of wreckage to another, at last I reached a cork raft. Soon the raft became so full it seemed as if she would sink if more came on board her. The crew for self-preservation had therefore to refuse to permit any others to climb aboard.

Hypothermia

Ships hurrying to the position where the *Titanic* had sunk pulled 333 bodies from the ocean. Nearly all of these victims, most wearing lifejackets, had died not of drowning but of hypothermia. This occurs when the body temperature drops too far below normal (36.5°C to 37.5°C or 98°F to 100°F) for the organs to continue to function. There was a rumour that passengers who had been drinking heavily survived longer in the cold water. In fact, the opposite was true. Alcohol increases blood flow to the skin, from where heat is lost more quickly.

Rescue and mutiny

Lifeboat 14, commanded by Fifth Officer Harold Lowe, was the only one to return to the scene and rescue survivors. They found four, all men, one of whom died of hypothermia after he was pulled into the boat. Lifeboat 4, commanded by Charles Lightoller, picked up seven people from the water close by, but two of them died that night. There was a mutiny in lifeboat 6 when Molly Brown and other women rejected the command of Quartermaster Robert Hitchens and rowed back to search for survivors. They were too late, and found only floating corpses.

THE *CARPATHIA*

At least one ship emerged from the *Titanic* tragedy with a reputation for courage, efficiency, and dedication. This was the 13,800-tonne Cunard liner, RMS *Carpathia*. Its captain, Arthur Rostron (1869–1940), became one of the great heroes of the rescue.

Signals received

On the night the *Titanic* sank, the emigrant ship *Carpathia* was sailing from New York to the Hungarian port of Fiume. Fortunately, as the vessel was now on the return leg of the journey, it was nowhere near its capacity of 2,550 passengers. As soon as the ship's radio operator picked up the *Titanic*'s distress signals shortly after midnight, he woke Captain Rostron with the alarming news.

Full steam ahead

Rostron had seen giant icebergs in the area, and knew that the great liner's call was no error or exaggeration. He ordered full speed ahead towards the *Titanic*'s last recorded position, about 93 km (58 miles) away. As the *Carpathia* could go no more than 17 knots (31 kph or 20 mph) and had to steer through dangerous ice, it was just after 3.30 a.m. by the time the ship reached its bleak destination.

▼ In a state of shock – survivors on the deck of the *Carpathia*, headed for New York.

▲ A fully loaded *Titanic* lifeboat being hauled aboard the *Carpathia*.

Rescue

Nothing. No sign of the *Titanic*, no boats, no debris. After searching for a while, Rostron ordered the *Carpathia*'s engines to stop, and all available crew to listen and look as the first cold light of dawn appeared on the eastern horizon. Shortly afterwards, a light! It was a flare from Lifeboat 2. Minutes later, the shivering, shocked survivors, many weeping with sorrow and relief, came aboard the *Carpathia* and confirmed the unbelievable truth – the *Titanic* had sunk.

Heading home

By 9 a.m., the *Carpathia* had located all the lifeboats and lifted their occupants to warmth and safety. His life-saving task complete, Rostron finally headed back to New York with the news that he had on board more than 700 survivors of what was then the worst maritime disaster the world had ever known.

❯ The 'unsinkable' Molly Brown presents a cup to Captain Arthur Henry Rostron of the *Carpathia* in recognition of his work in rescuing *Titanic* survivors.

DISASTER!

Thanks to radio messages collected and re-broadcast from Cape Race, Canada, and from the *Carpathia*, news of the *Titanic* disaster began to get out early on the morning of Monday 15 April. Across the world, newspaper headlines screamed out the incredible story.

Questions ...

Everyone wanted information. In Liverpool, the headquarters of the White Star Line was surrounded by reporters, and anxious friends and relatives of passengers who had set sail on the ill-fated liner. Employees, worried about meeting the crowd face to face, called down the limited news they had from first-floor windows.

As the shocking facts sank in, the questions began. These mostly fell into two categories. First, how many survivors were there and what were their names? Second, why had such a terrible disaster happened, and who was to blame?

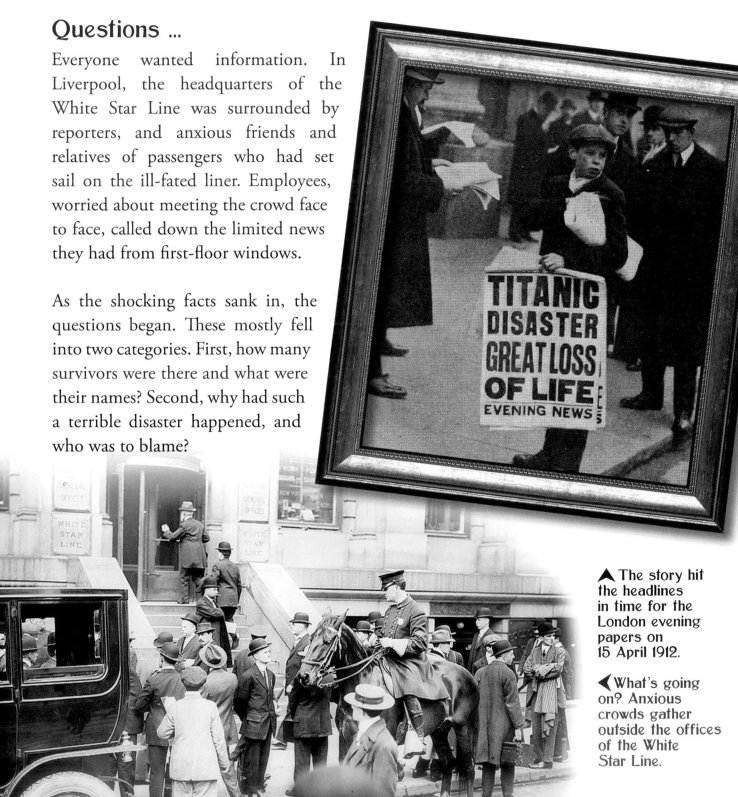

▲ The story hit the headlines in time for the London evening papers on 15 April 1912.

◀ What's going on? Anxious crowds gather outside the offices of the White Star Line.

... and answers

To this day there remains some uncertainty about the exact number and identity of persons rescued from the *Titanic*. This is because the ports of Southampton, Cherbourg, and Queenstown were unable to come up with precise figures for the numbers of passengers and crew who had embarked and disembarked there. The only exact record lay at the bottom of the Atlantic Ocean. Explanations for the tragedy, many wildly inaccurate, were flying around even before the *Carpathia* reached New York. One of the most popular was that the ship was travelling too fast. For this, blame was laid at the feet of Captain Smith and J. Bruce Ismay, chairman of the White Star Line.

Reception

The *Carpathia* reached America on 18 April. Steaming into New York harbour in the dark, the ship dropped off the *Titanic's* lifeboats at the White Star Line pier before tying up at pier 54. The arrival was greeted by a huge crowd of relatives, friends, press, and helpers. Many survivors, particularly those emigrating to the USA, had lost all their worldly possessions as well as friends and family. With remarkable kindness and generosity, a number of New York organisations raised money, organised food and shelter, and helped the shattered, bedraggled survivors in many other ways. Help and comfort were needed on the other side of the Atlantic, too. A local newspaper estimated that 1,000 Southampton families had suffered directly as a result of the sinking.

▼ Official confirmation sent to the government in London that the *Titanic* had sunk.

M14488

LIVERPOOL, April 16th, 1912.

J. Howell, K.C.B.
Marine Department, Board of Trade,
7, Whitehall Gardens,
London. S.W.

Dear Sir,

Further to our communication of yesterday we were extremely sorry to have to send you the following wire this morning :-

"Referring telegram yesterday 'Titanic' deeply grieved "say that during night we received word steamer foundered "about 675 souls mostly women and children saved".

which we now beg to confirm.

Yours faithfully,

For ISMAY. IMRIE & CO:

CLASSIFIED

49

SURVIVORS AND VICTIMS

The *Carpathia* picked up 710 or 711 passengers from the *Titanic's* boats. Although sources disagree on the exact number, they accept that only 705 made it back alive to New York. The other five or six were either dead when taken from the lifeboats, or died on the *Carpathia*. All were buried at sea.

Bodies in the sea

Once the surviving passengers had been listed and taken care of, the grisly business of accounting for those missing could begin. First, bodies had to be recovered from the sea. Two Canadian ships, especially chartered for the purpose, found 324 floating corpses. Passing vessels picked up another 13 bodies. Of these, 128 were buried at sea, and the rest brought back to Halifax, in the Canadian province of Nova Scotia. We know that 150 were buried in Halifax, and 59 laid to rest elsewhere. Victims' families were angry that the White Star Line would not pay to have the bodies of their relatives brought back home.

▼ Rescued *Titanic* crew members were given dry clothes when they arrived in New York.

Passenger Category	Percent Saved	Percent Lost	Number Saved	Number Lost	Number Aboard
Children, First Class	100.00	0.00	6	0	6
Children, Second Class	100.00	0.00	24	0	24
Children, Third Class	34.18	65.82	27	52	79
Women, First Class	97.22	2.78	140	4	144
Women, Crew	86.96	13.04	20	3	23
Women, Second Class	86.02	13.98	80	13	93
Women, Third Class	46.06	53.94	76	89	165
Men, First Class	32.57	67.43	57	118	175
Men, Crew	21.69	78.31	192	693	885
Men, Second Class	8.33	91.67	14	154	168
Men, Third Class	16.23	83.77	75	387	462
Total	31.97	68.03	711	1513	2224

Who survived?

The chart above, produced by the British inquiry into the disaster, gives a breakdown of the casualty figure. The passenger and crew numbers are not entirely accurate but a number of conclusions stand out.

- Children had the best chance of survival, followed by women, then men.

- The more a passenger had paid for their ticket, the more likely they were to survive. This was partly because first- and second-class accommodation was nearer the boat deck. However, there were people who thought that some officers loading the lifeboats may have considered wealthy passengers more 'important' than poorer ones. Less than 25 per cent of all third-class passengers survived.

- The survival rate among male crew members was slightly better than that for second- and third-class male passengers, because crew were required to manage the lifeboats.

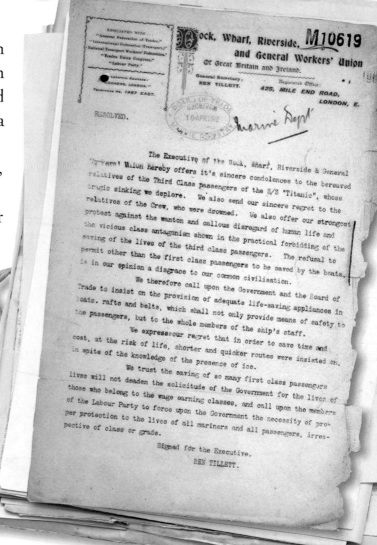

▲ Ben Tillett, a famous trade union leader, complained that first-class passengers appeared to have had priority in the lifeboats.

THE INQUIRY BEGINS

Plans for an inquiry into the reasons for the *Titanic* disaster were well advanced in the USA before the *Carpathia* reached New York on 18 April. The US Senate quickly set up a committee for the investigation. The man chosen to head it, Senator William Alden Smith, had already made a name for himself as a campaigner for greater safety on the US railways.

Facts and figures

In order to speak to the British crew members before they returned to the UK, the American committee of inquiry had to move fast. Meeting first in New York's Waldorf-Astoria hotel (partly owned by J.J. Astor, who died on the *Titanic*) on 18 April, it questioned witnesses for 17 days. The committee called 82 individuals before it, and the report of their evidence filled 1,100 pages.

▼ US Senator William Alden Smith (1859–1932) was known by the British press as 'Watertight Smith', because he misunderstood the purpose of the watertight compartments in the *Titanic*.

Conclusions

Smith's report noted that the disaster had many causes. Some, such as the inadequate number of lifeboats carried by the *Titanic*, were the result of administrative errors. Others, such as the ship's speed and the cancellation of the lifeboat drill, were due to human error. From his questions, it was clear that Senator Smith wondered whether Captain Smith had been travelling faster than he knew was wise, because of instructions from Ismay.

> "
> This excerpt from the US Senate report sent to the British embassy in Washington clearly states the causes found for the *Titanic* disaster:
>
> *The report … attacks with some vehemence the notion of the Commander of the* Californian *and lays considerable stress on the small heed that was given to the warnings of the presence of ice in the track of the* Titanic*, while the method of filling and launching the lifeboats is also censured. It further condemns the hasty inspection of the vessel by the Board of Trade Inspector during her trials.*
> "

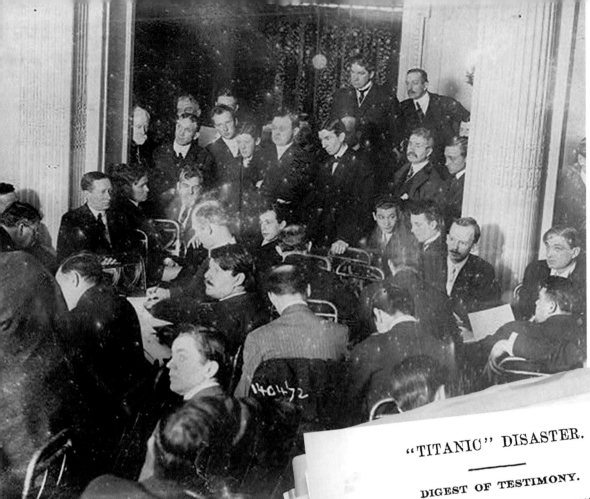

Recommendations

Smith's committee came up with a number of clear and sensible recommendations to prevent similar tragedies in the future. These included equipping vessels with enough lifeboats to hold everyone on board. Shortly after the *Titanic* went down, the crew of its sister ship, the *Olympic*, refused to sail until extra lifeboats were provided.

The committee's proposed measures also included compulsory lifeboat drills, double-layered hulls, improved watertight bulkheads, and 24-hour supervision of a radio on all ships.

"TITANIC" DISASTER.

DIGEST OF TESTIMONY.

ALARM:
"No alarm sounded," Maj. Peuchen.
"The alarm bell for accidents rang outside of our door," Fireman Taylor.
"The bedroom steward's duty to awaken passengers when an accident occurs," Steward Wheelton.
"A sort of a general order was passed around." Steward Cunningham.
"Tell all the other bedroom stewards to assemble their passengers on the boat deck," order of purser to Steward Etches.
" * * * to arouse the passengers," Passenger Stengel.
"I heard the order given
Whether passengers were notified or not, "I have no absolute knowledge," Officer Lightoller.

C. Q. D. CALLS:
Cape Race hears Titanic's C. Q. D. at 10.25 p. m., New York time.
Mount Temple hears C. Q. D. at 10.25 p. m., New York time.
"Purely and simply an accident," Mount Temple replies, but Titanic can not read.
"The Frankfurt was the first one to answer * * * , as far as I know immediately," Bride.
Frankfurt heard, 10.40, New York time.
Calling Titanic to say Cape Cod was sending to him.
Carpathia "providentially" got the Titanic's C. Q. D.
Carpathia was second to answer.
Carpathia answers 10.35, New York time.
Olympic and Baltic respond.
Caronia hears Titanic.
Mount Temple last hears 11.47.
Baltic last hears, "Our engine room getting flooded," about 11.45 p. m.
Carpathia last hears engine room getting flooded.
Virginia last hears signals blurred and ending abruptly 12.27.
Olympic last hears Titanic about 11.43–45, New York time.

COLLISION, EFFECT OF:
"As though a heavy wave," Passenger Peuchen.
"Just a slight grinding noise," Lookout Fleet.
"A sound like the ship coming to anchor * * * just a little vibration," Officer Pitman.
"Slight impact," Officer Boxhall.
"Did not waken me," Officer Lowe.
"A slight shock, a slight trembling, and a grinding sound," Officer Lightoller.
"The grinding noise along the ship's bottom," Quartermaster Hichens.
"I felt a slight jar," Quartermaster Rowe.
"A long, grinding sound," Quartermaster Olliver.
"Awakened by a shock as if it was the dropping of a propeller," Steward Wheelton.
"A noise like a cable running out," Seaman Moore.
"I heard something just the same as a ship going through a lot of loose ice," Seaman Jones.
"Only a slight jar, a grinding noise," Lookout Symons.
"I heard this slight shock," Steward Hardy.
"A slight jar, a gradual jar; I did not think it was anything at all," Steward Hardy.

1147

FURTHER INVESTIGATION

Compared with the snappy American inquiry, the British process was drawn-out and formal. It began on 2 May 1912 and, after 36 days of questioning, the final report was issued on 30 July. At the time, and in the years that followed, many felt the conclusions to be rather feeble. In particular, when so many errors had been made, people questioned why no individuals were held responsible.

Strange surroundings

The British inquiry opened in the former armoury of the Scottish Rifles regiment. The building was chosen for its size, as it was able to hold several hundred spectators. On the first day, however, only around 100 members of the public turned up.

In addition, about 100 representatives each from the press and the legal profession were present at the inquiry. Many complained that not a word of the proceedings could be heard because of the cavernous echo. Before them stood a scale model of the *Titanic*, 6 m (20 ft) long. A huge chart of the North Atlantic region hung on the wall.

▼ Silence in court! The British inquiry into the disaster was conducted like a trial, with a judge in charge.

Court of law

Unlike the US inquiry, the British investigation was conducted like a court of law, dealing with 26 precise questions. The Liverpool-born judge, Charles Bingham (Lord Mersey), was in charge. He had retired two years earlier, and had a reputation for being a grumpy old man. He was criticised in some of the press for being more interested in preventing further disasters than finding out what had gone wrong in this one.

Recommendations

The recommendations of the British inquiry were very similar to those suggested in the USA, although more detailed. They said, for instance, that lifeboats should have their own motor, and that vessels should be inspected while under construction. Another idea was that lookouts should have regular eye tests. American businesses were less keen on regulations of this sort. They tended to believe they should be free to do their work without interference from the government.

▲ The Journal of Commerce published a book that summarised every day of the *Titanic* inquiry, and gave details about its findings.

▶ Lord Mersey (1840–1929), who suffered from deafness, shot to fame for his handling of the *Titanic* inquiry. Some said he could have been more hard-hitting in his verdict.

> The final conclusion of the British inquiry was a clear one:
>
> *The Court, having carefully inquired into the circumstances of the above mentioned shipping casualty, finds, for the reasons appearing in the annex hereto, that the loss of the said ship was due to collision with an iceberg, brought about by the excessive speed at which the ship was being navigated.*

WHY DID THE *TITANIC* SINK?

The American and British inquiries of 1912 may have been hasty, but they were surprisingly thorough. Both inquiries concluded that the *Titanic* sank not because of one single cause, but because of a combination of many factors. Some of these factors led to the ship colliding with an iceberg. Others led to it sinking as a result of the collision.

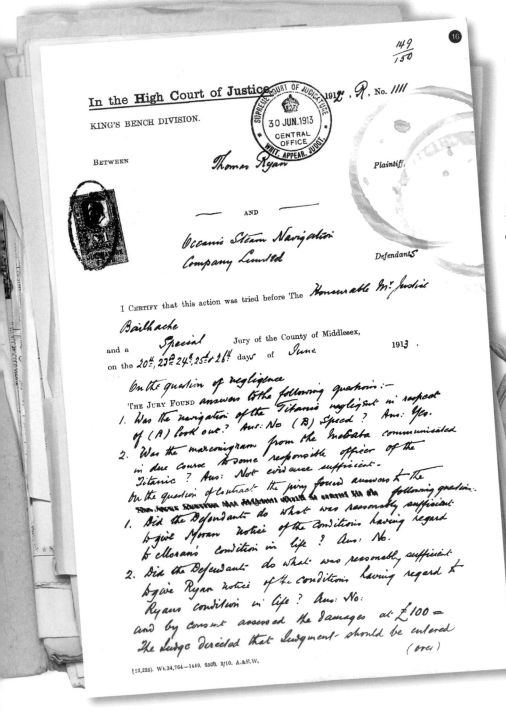

Speed

The *Titanic* hit the iceberg essentially because it was going too fast in dangerous waters at night. Its speed was not unusual for a large liner on that route, because it was assumed that an iceberg large enough to cause damage would be spotted in time to take measures to avoid it.

The failure to pick up the *Californian*'s radio warnings may have played a part, too. The *Titanic* might have taken different and quicker action, although it is not clear that this would have prevented the collision.

◀ Nowadays, disasters usually lead to claims for compensation – but not in 1912, despite occasional threats to sue for negligence, as this letter reveals.

▲ After hearing of the *Titanic*'s sinking, people in Bournemouth made the first memorial to the *Titanic* - a temporary shrine on the sandy beach.

Construction

A ship in use today would not sink as the result of a similar collision. Lessons learnt from the sinking of the *Titanic* and other shipping disasters have helped to make ships today stronger and safer than ever before.

Had the *Titanic*'s hull been double-layered, and its watertight compartments closed at the top, events would have played out very differently. Welded joints rather than riveted ones might have helped, too, as might have larger pumps and a larger rudder.

Over-confidence

Another important factor in the disaster was the over-confidence of those in charge of the *Titanic*. Technological advances in shipbuilding led some to underestimate the destructive power of nature. This attitude is clear in the words of Captain Smith, reported in the *New York Times* on 16 April 1912:

> *I cannot imagine any condition which would cause a ship to founder. I cannot conceive of any vital disaster happening to this vessel. Modern shipbuilding has gone beyond that.*

Finding the *Titanic*

For 73 years, evidence of the *Titanic* disaster was based solely on old documents, photographs, and personal memories. The remains of the great ship itself remained lost. Then, in 1985, a French–American team's high-powered sonar picked up what everyone had been waiting for.

Discoveries

Finally, the lost wreck of the *Titanic* had been uncovered. The depth of the wreckage – roughly 4 km (2.5 miles) underwater – was as expected. However, the broken ship was found around 21 km (13 miles) from where it was previously believed to lie. Soon after the *Titanic*'s rediscovery, a remotely controlled submersible and then a staffed vehicle went down to photograph the wreck.

Answers

Contrary to what many survivors and both inquiries had said, these pictures showed that the *Titanic* really did break into two pieces before it sank. The two sections lay 600 m (1,970 feet) apart on the ocean floor. The bow section, buried 18 m (60 ft) in silt, was relatively intact. The stern section, which sank with air trapped inside, was badly crushed by the weight of the water as it went down.

Enduring memories

Experts say that within 20–30 years, the *Titanic*'s rusting steel hull will dissolve into the surrounding mud. The final remnants of the great ship will then disappear for ever. However, although the ship itself will no longer be with us, RMS *Titanic* will live on in the memories and stories of that terrible night.

The Titanic *is the grave of 1,513 unfortunate people who needn't have died, and [as] such ... should be left there in memory of them.*

Eva Hart, *Titanic* survivor, speaking in 1987.

GLOSSARY

Note – Many of the words listed here (*bridge*, for example) have more than one meaning. The definition given here is for the meaning used in this book.

annex additional material

boat deck deck where lifeboats are stored

bow front of a ship

bridge command and control centre of a ship

bugle brass musical instrument, often used in ceremonies

bulkhead wall within a ship's hull

cargo goods carried on board a ship

chambermaid maid who looks after a woman in her bedroom

crow's nest high point on a ship where the lookouts are positioned

debris objects and fragments left scattered, often after a disaster

dignitary person who is considered to hold a high position in society

disembark get off a boat

drill practise run of an emergency procedure

embark get on a boat

emigrant someone leaving a country to go and live in another one

hold area of a ship where luggage and cargo are kept

hull main body of a ship, divided by decks, with the keel at the bottom

hypothermia dangerous loss of body heat

immigrant someone entering a country to live there permanently

keel strong backbone running along the very bottom of a ship

knot speed of one nautical mile (1.8 km, 1.15 ordinary miles) per hour

latitude imaginary lines running horizontally round the earth. The best known is the one round the middle – the Equator

lifejacket emergency jacket that floats and prevents its wearer from drowning

liner large ship that carries passengers from one port to another

longitude imaginary lines that run up and down the earth from pole to pole

maiden voyage ship's first working voyage

negligence failure to take proper care, resulting in injury or damage

opium an addictive drug

ornate highly decorated

paddlewheel large wheels, like waterwheels, that were used to drive powered ships before the use of propellers

pier part of a dock or harbour sticking out from the shore – ships can be tied up to it

port sailor's word for 'left'; place where ships stop to load and unload; sweet wine

promenade deck spacious deck where passengers can take exercise

purser officer on a ship in charge of passengers' luggage, tickets and onboard financial matters

quay part of a harbour or dock nearest to a ship, to which vessels are tied up for loading and unloading

radar electronic device for locating objects – such as ships or aircraft – at a great distance

radical wanting serious change

rivet metal bolt that joins two plates together without the use of a nut

RMS Royal Mail Ship

rudder moveable plate at the stern of a ship, used for steering

screw propeller

shipyard place where ships are constructed

silt loose dirt on the seabed

slipway ramp down which a newly built ship first slides into the sea

sonar electronic device for finding objects under the surface of water

starboard sailor's word for 'right'

stern back of a ship

SS Steam Ship

submersible machine for exploring below the surface of the water

superstructure upper part of a ship rising above the hull

telegram electronic message using telephone landline

tender small boat for ferrying passengers to and from a larger one

transatlantic across the Atlantic Ocean

turbine type of engine that uses fans rather than pistons

valet manservant

ventilation providing fresh air to the inside of a building or structure

weld join together by melting metal in a very hot flame

winch large winding machine

windlass machine – powered by hand or by an engine – for pulling up a heavy anchor rope or chain

wireless radio

FIND OUT MORE

Books

101 Things You Thought You Knew About the Titanic ... But Didn't!
by Eloise Aston & Tim Maltin
(Beautiful Books, 2010)

RMS Titanic Manual: 1909–1912 Olympic Class
by David Hutchings & Richard de Kerbrech
(Haynes, 2011)

The Story of the Titanic as Told by its Survivors
by J Winocour, ed.
(Dover, 1950 and reprints)

Titanic
by Anton Gill
(Channel 4 Books, 2010)

Titanic: Death on the Water
by Tom and Tony Bradman
(A & C Black and National Archives, 2011)
A fictional retelling of the story of the *Titanic*

Titanic: the Disaster that Shocked the World!
by Mark Dubowski
(DK Readers, 1998)

The Titanic Experience: The Legend of the Unsinkable Ship
by Beau Riffenburgh
(Carlton, 2009)

Websites and exhibitions

The National Archives have podcasts relating to the *Titanic*, available to download free from their website (links below) and from iTunes:
www.nationalarchives.gov.uk/podcasts/titanic-the-official-story.htm
www.nationalarchives.gov.uk/podcasts/titanic-lives.htm

There is an excellent series of interviews with *Titanic* survivors on
www.bbc.co.uk/archive/titanic

RMS *Titanic* Inc. owns the wreck and has salvage rights to it.
The organisation tours exhibitions of its material around the world:
www.rmstitanic.net

There are also good displays at the National Maritime Museum in Greenwich:
www.nmm.ac.uk

The Merseyside Maritime Museum also has content relating to the *Titanic*:
www.liverpoolmuseums.org.uk/maritime

ⒶThe National Archives

The National Archives is the UK government's official archive, containing over 1,000 years of history. They give detailed guidance to government departments and the public sector on information management, and advise others about the care of historical archives.
www.nationalarchives.gov.uk

National Archives Picture Acknowledgements and Catalogue References

p8-9 MT 15/504 pt.1. Blue deck plans for the Titanic.
p29 BT 350. ID cards for crew members Charles John Joughin and William George White.
p36 COPY 1/565/56461. Photo of Jack Phillips.
p37 MT 9/920C/527 and MT 9/920C/528. Record of telegrams between Titanic and Birma.
p39 MT 9/920C/525 and MT 9/920C/532. Telegrams between Titanic and Birma.
p44-45 COPY 1/566. Lifeboat D reaching the Carpathian.
p49 MT 9/920C/327. Confirmation letter that the Titanic sank.
p51 MT 9/920A/1/106. A letter of complaint from union leader Ben Tillett.
p53 MT 9/920 G. Digest of US inquiry into Titanic sinking (1912).
p56 J 54/1548. No. R 1111. Letter about suing for negligence, dated 30 Jun 1913 (UK).
p57 COPY 1/566/56550. Sand memorial to Titanic victims on Bournemouth beach.

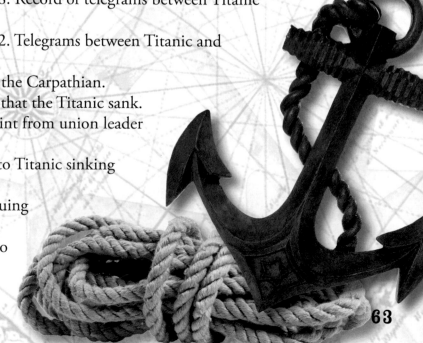

INDEX

Picture credits